Super Safari 1

Activity Book

Herbert Puchta Günter Gerngross Peter Lewis-Jones

Shaftesbury Road, Cambridge CB2 8EA, United Kingdom

One Liberty Plaza, 20th Floor, New York, NY 10006, USA

477 Williamstown Road, Port Melbourne, VIC 3207, Australia

314–321, 3rd Floor, Plot 3, Splendor Forum, Jasola District Centre, New Delhi – 110025, India

103 Penang Road, #05-06/07, Visioncrest Commercial, Singapore 238467

Cambridge University Press & Assessment is a department of the University of Cambridge.

We share the University's mission to contribute to society through the pursuit of education, learning and research at the highest international levels of excellence.

www.cambridge.org
Information on this title: www.cambridge.org/9781107476691

First published 2015

40 39 38 37 36 35 34 33 32 31 30 29 28

Printed by Ashford Colour Press Ltd

A catalogue record for this publication is available from the British Library

ISBN 978-1-107-47669-1 Activity Book Level 1
ISBN 978-1-107-47667-7 Pupil's Book with DVD-ROM Level 1
ISBN 978-1-107-47670-7 Teacher's Book Level 1
ISBN 978-1-107-47687-5 Teacher's DVD Level 1
ISBN 978-1-107-47673-8 Class Audio CDs Level 1
ISBN 978-1-107-47679-0 Flashcards Level 1
ISBN 978-1-107-47682-0 Presentation Plus DVD-ROM Level 1
ISBN 978-1-107-47729-2 Posters Level 1
ISBN 978-1-107-47732-2 Puppet

Additional resources for this publication at www.cambridge.org/supersafari

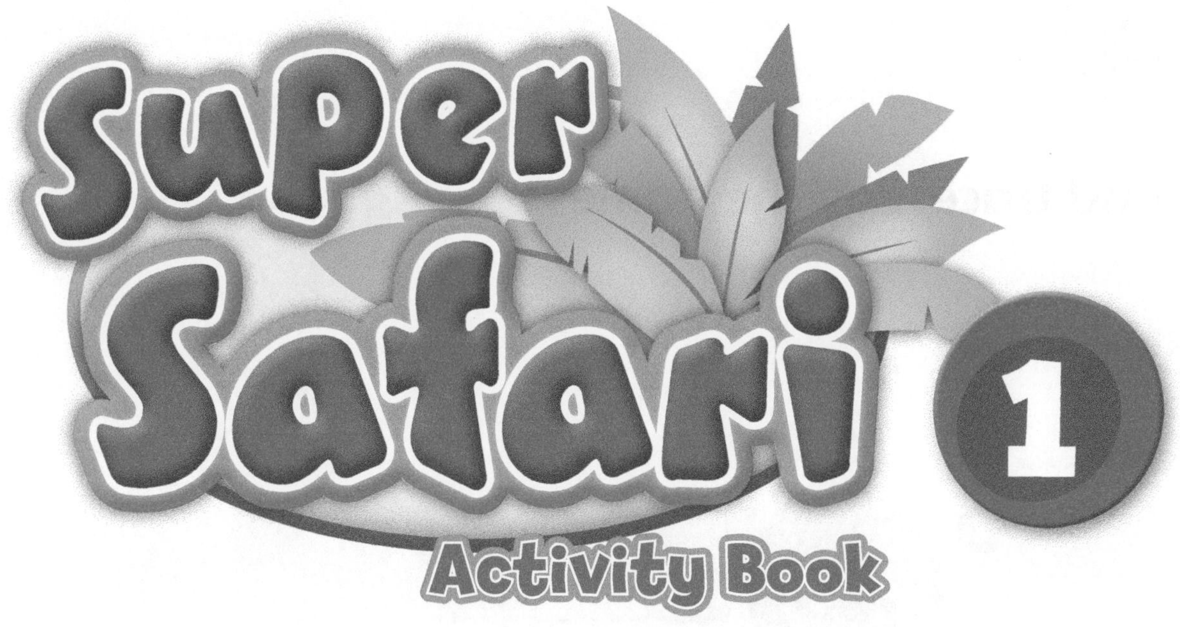
Super Safari 1
Activity Book

Hello!

1 **Look and trace. Say the names.**

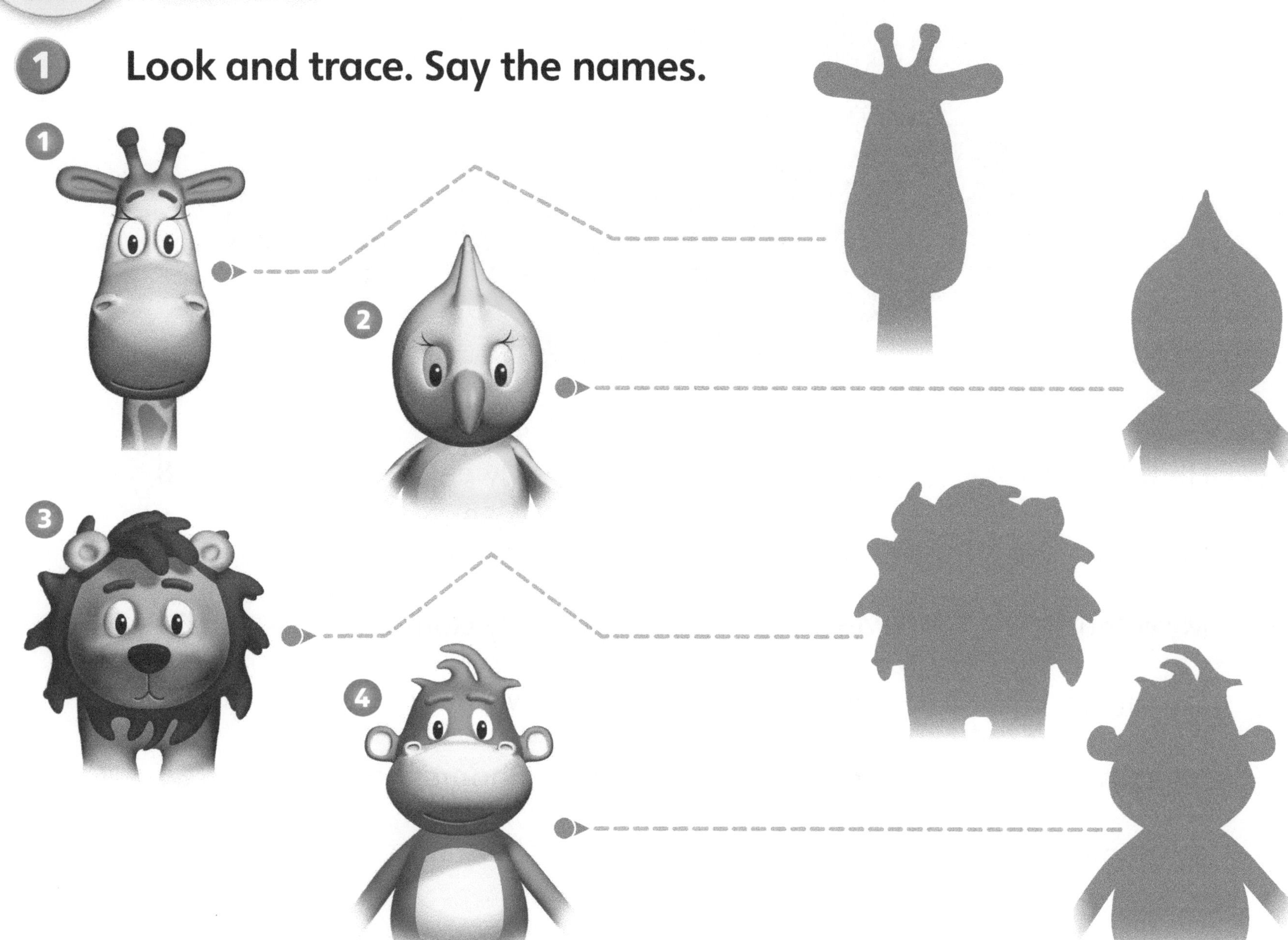

2 Draw yourself. Say the sentence.

Listen and circle.

4 Say the names. Colour the circles.

1

2

3

4
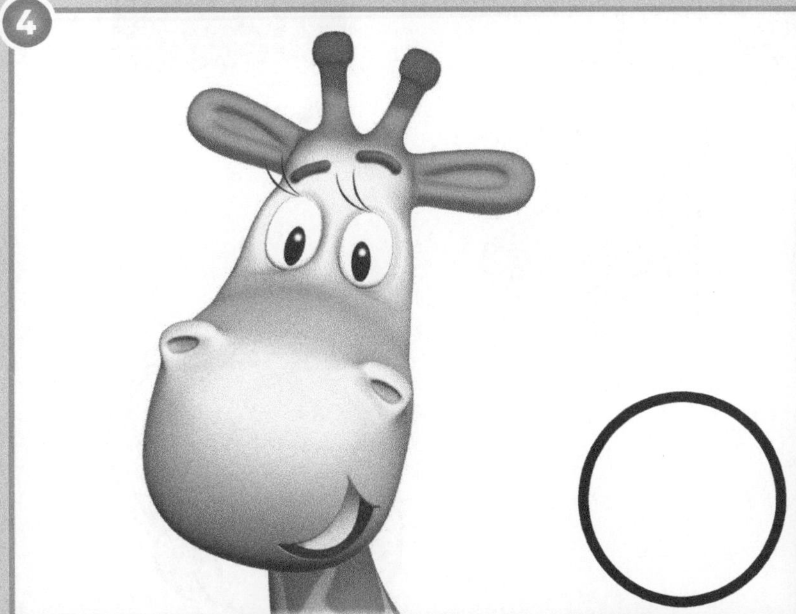

1 My class

1 Look and match. Say the words.

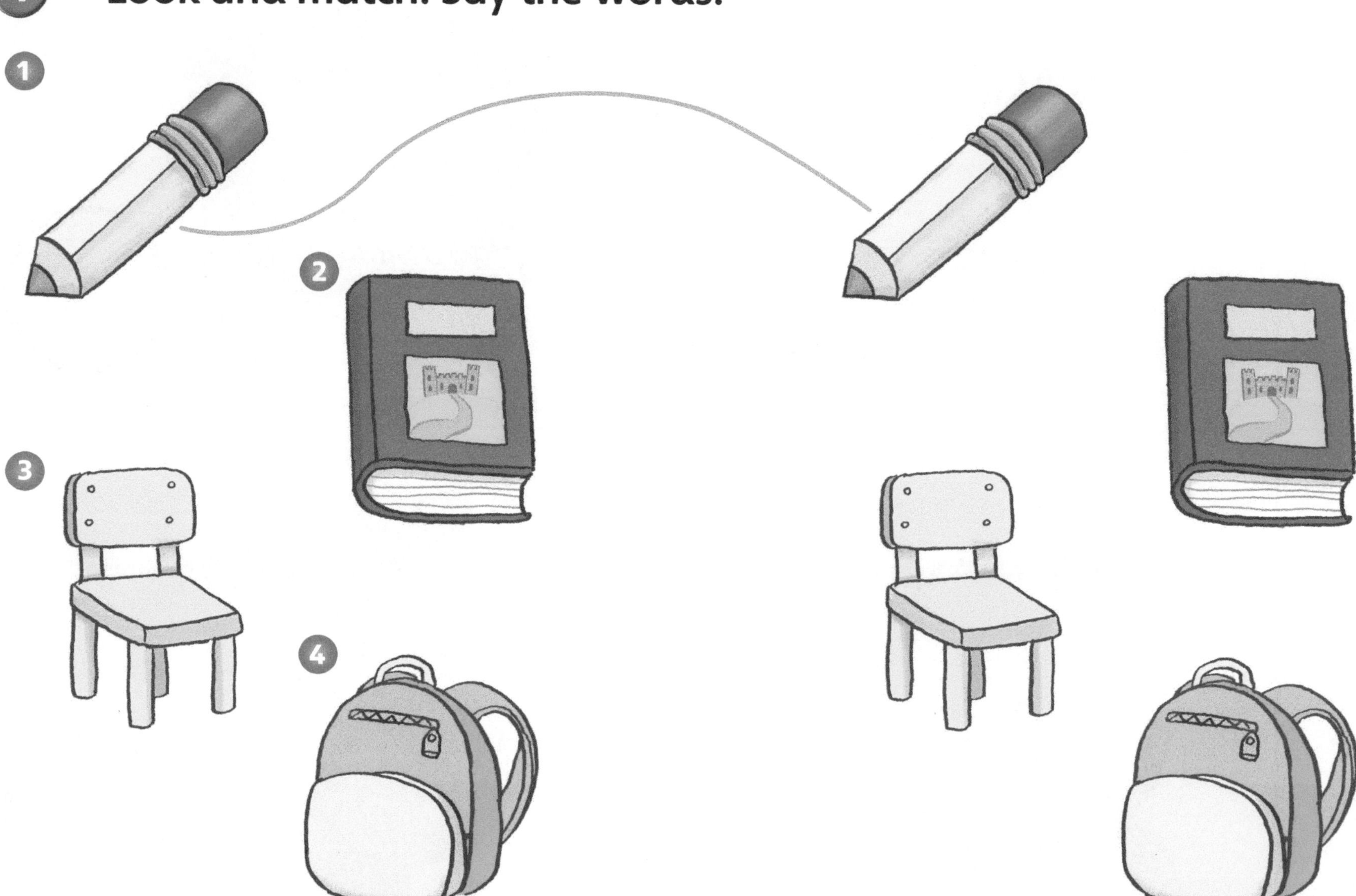

Listen and join the dots. Say the sentence.

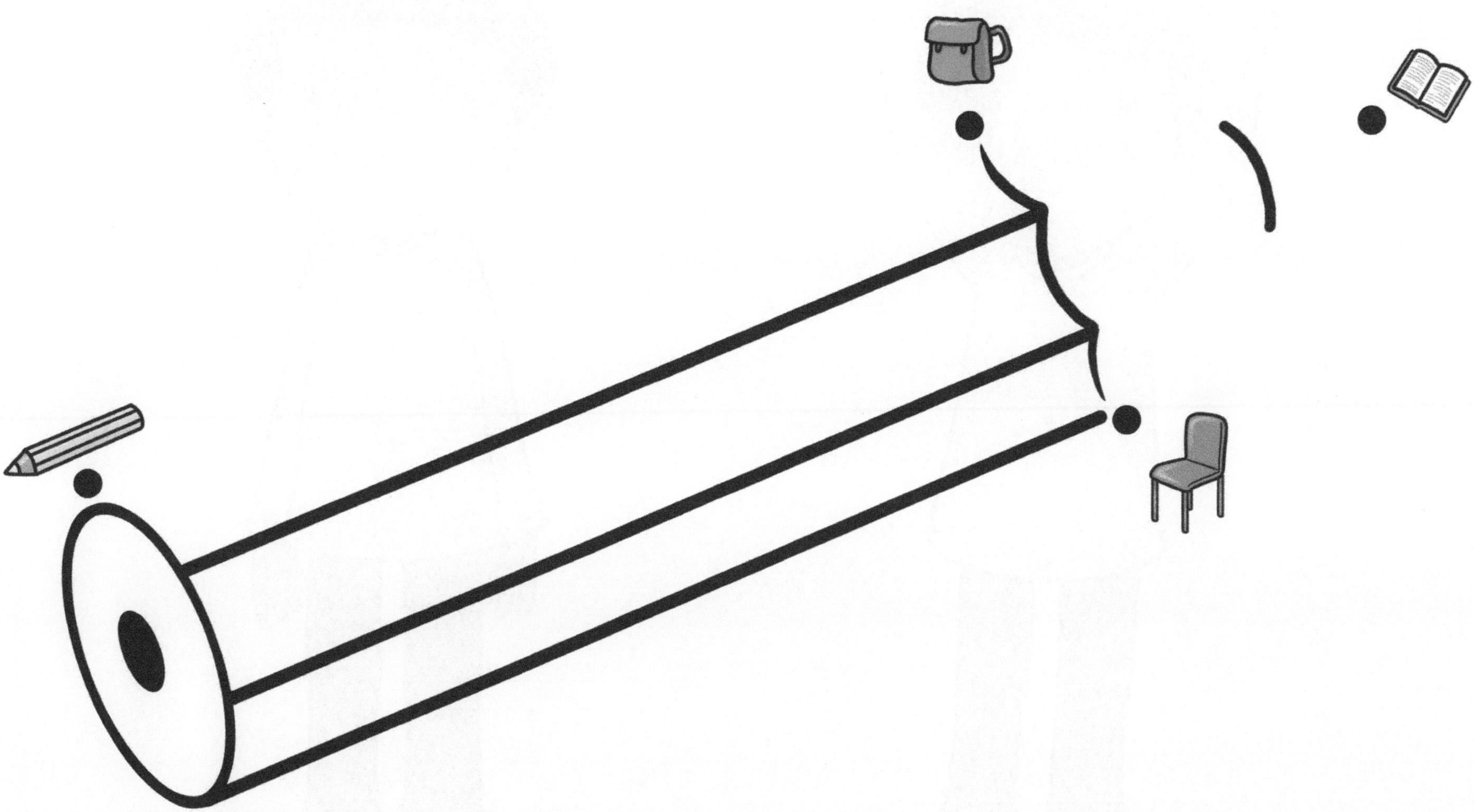

Listen and circle.

4 Follow the path.

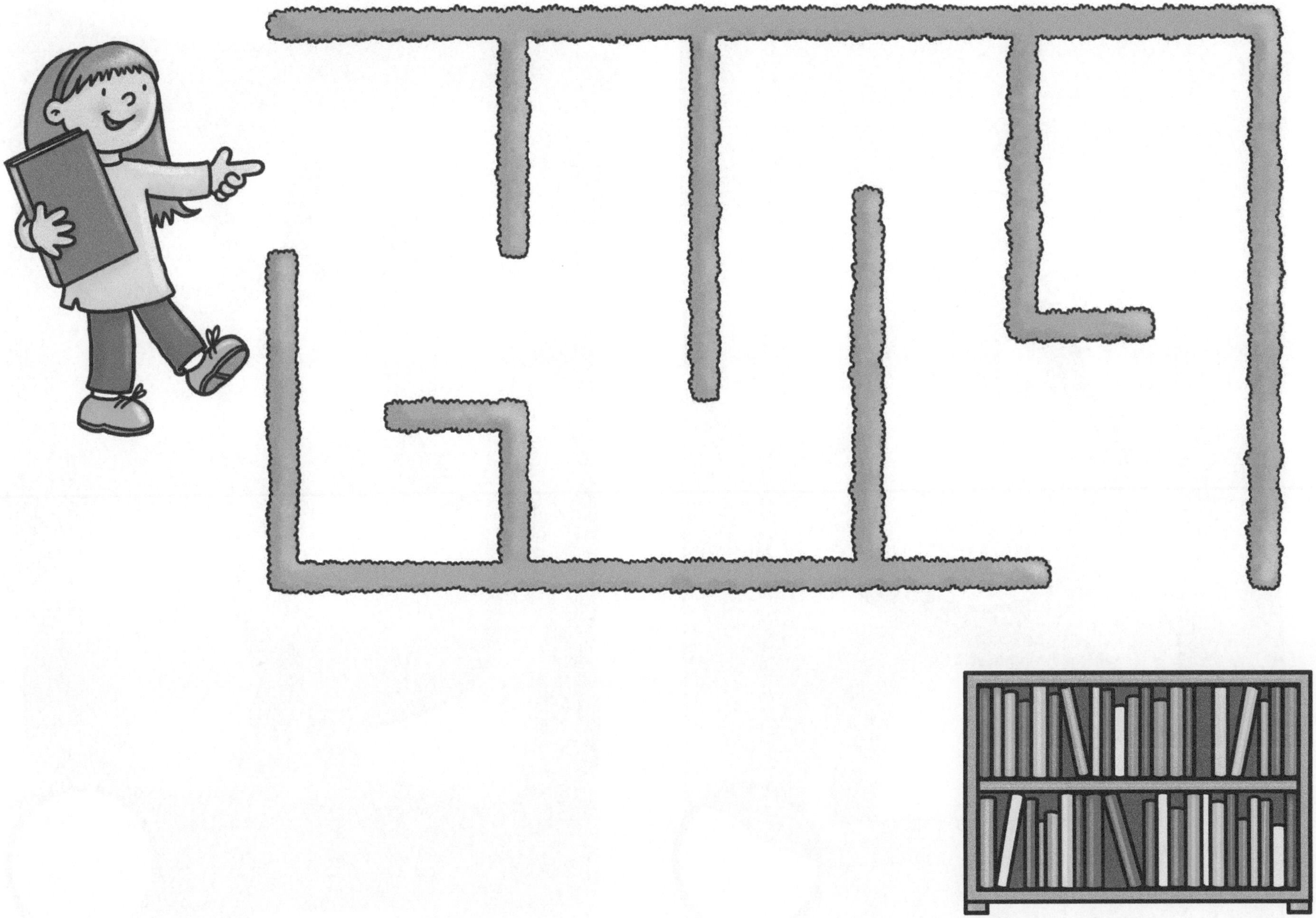

5 Listen and colour the correct circle.

6 Complete the face (☺). Colour the picture.

7 Make a model of yourself.

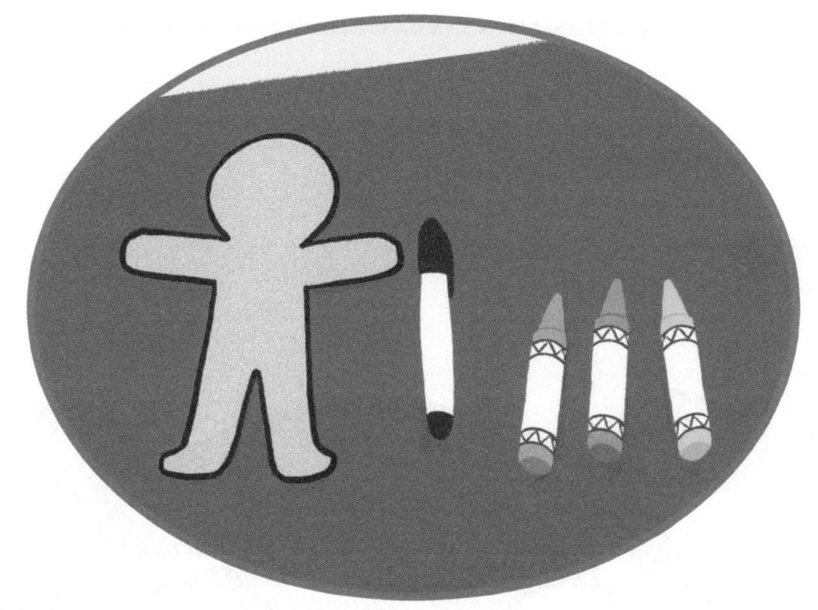

1

2

3

8 Say the words. Colour the circles.

1

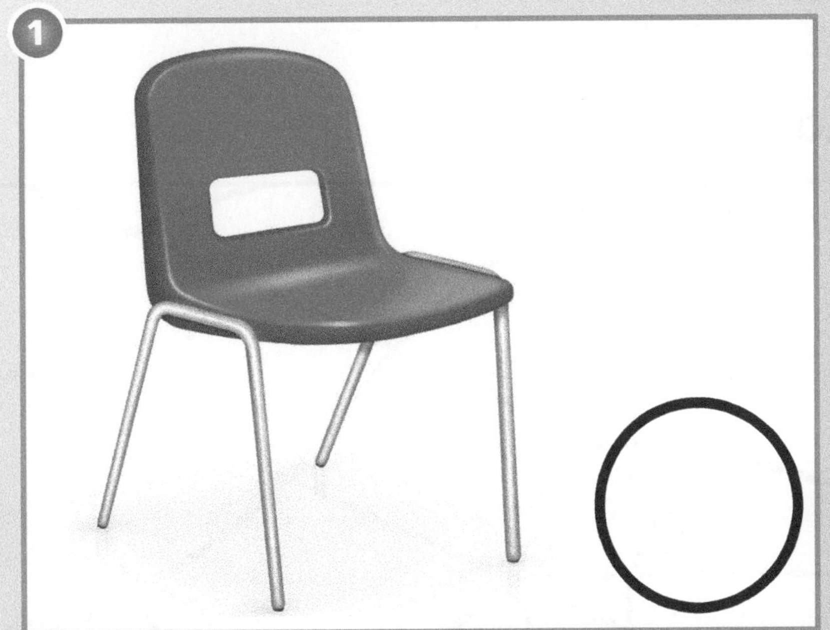

2

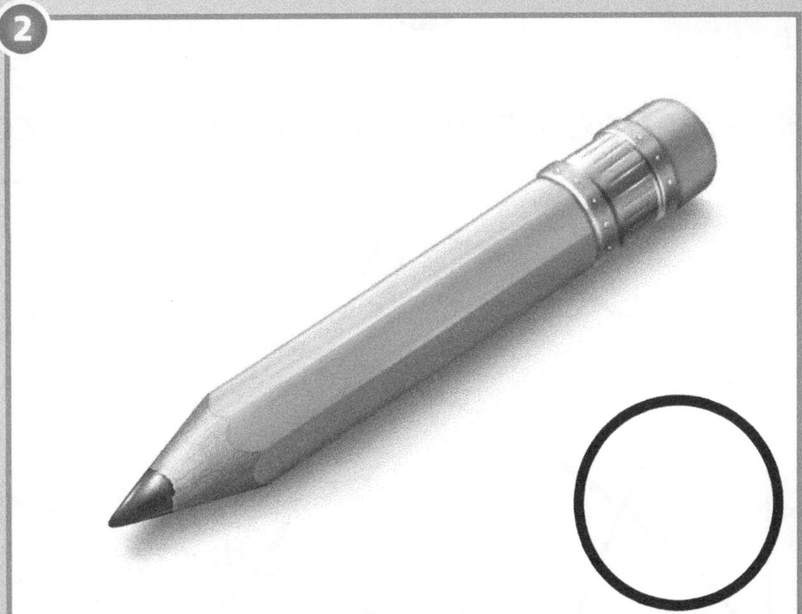

3

4

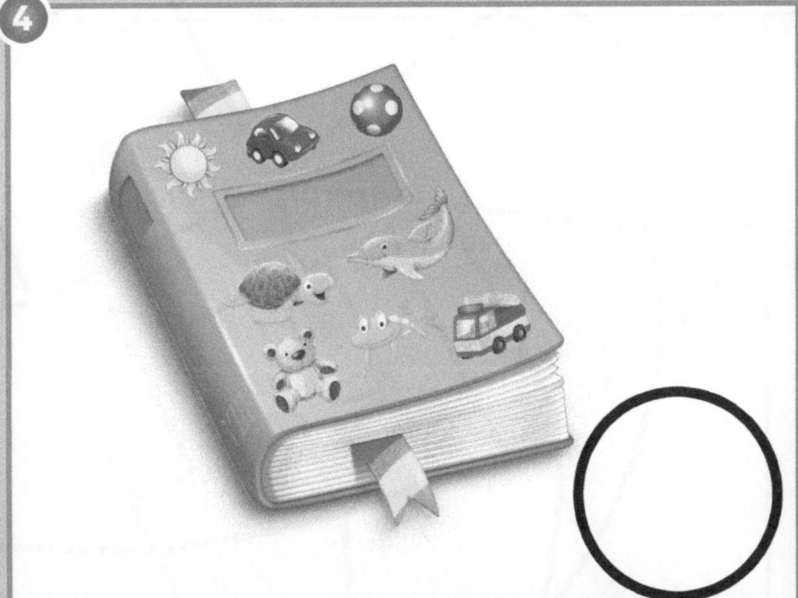

2 My colours

1 Look and colour. Say the colours.

red, blue, green, yellow

2 Look and colour. Say the sentences.

3 CD1 24 Listen and circle.

4 CD1 27 Listen again and colour.

Listen and colour the correct circle.

6 Complete the face (☺). Colour the picture.

7 Make a mixed-colour painting.

1

2
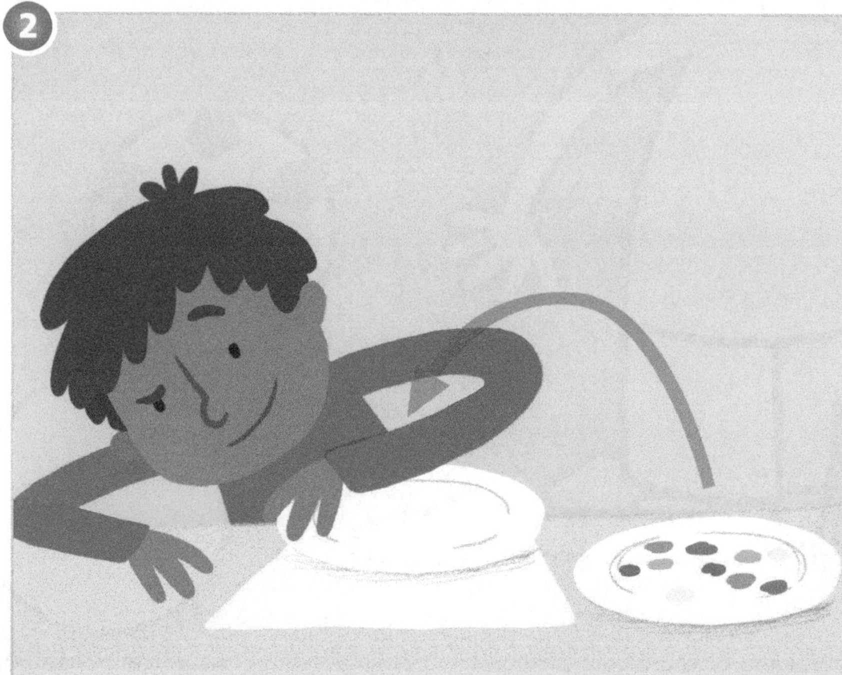

3

8 Say the colours. Colour the circles.

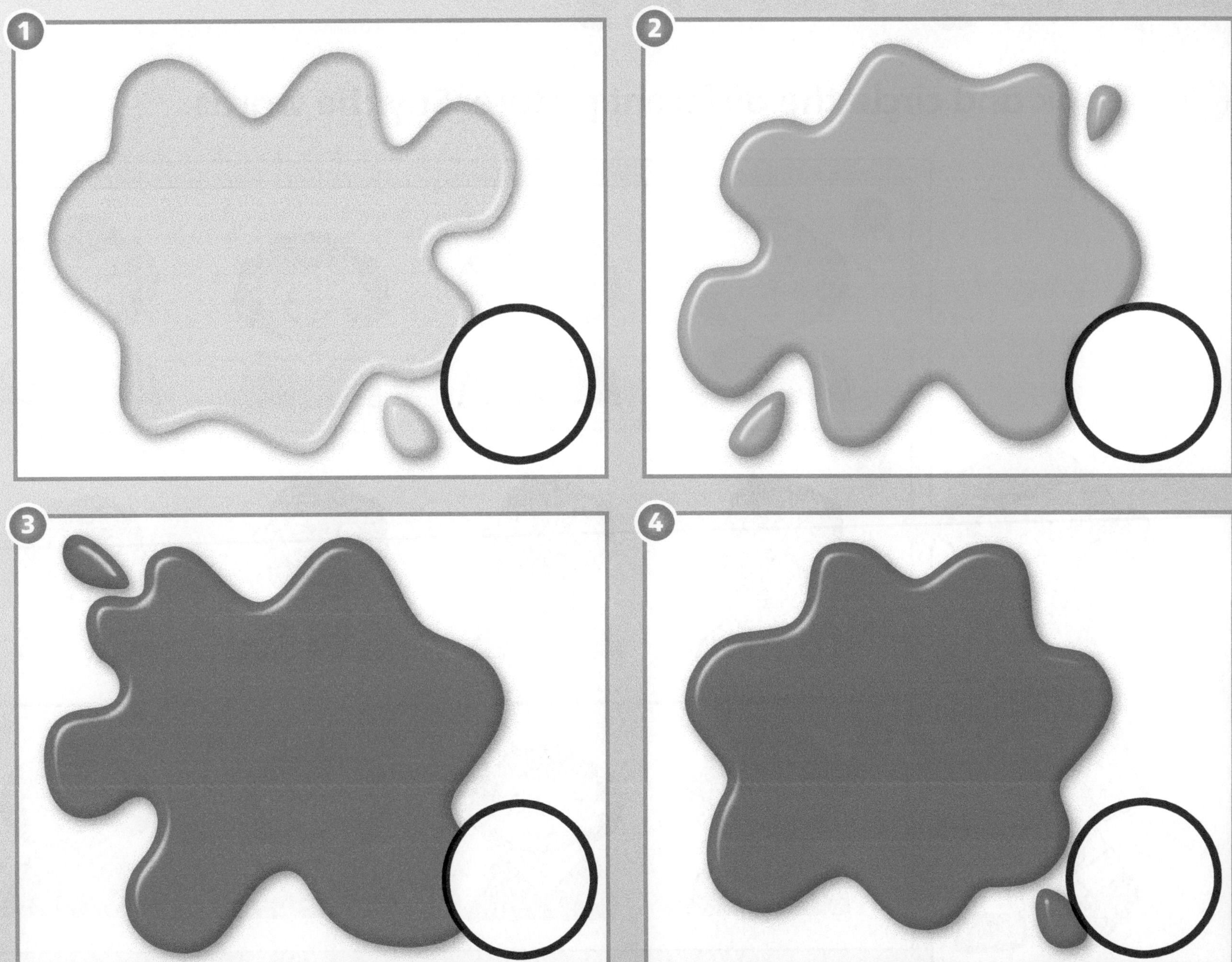

3 My family

1 **Look and circle the different picture. Say the words.**

2 **Draw a family member. Say the sentence.**

3 Listen and circle.

Listen and match.

5 Listen and colour the correct circle.

6 Complete the face (☺). Colour the picture.

7 Make a rocking chicken.

1

2

3

8 Say the words. Colour the circles.

1

2

3

4

4 My toys

1 CD1 46 **Listen and colour. Say the toys.**

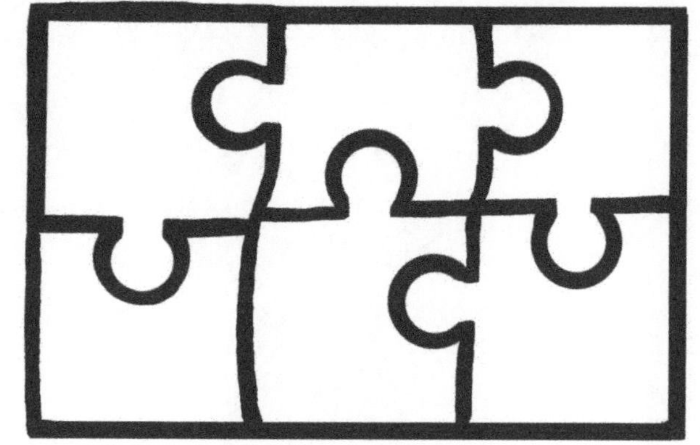

2 Draw a toy. Say the sentence.

3 CD1 50 Listen and circle.

4 CD1 53 Listen again. Trace and colour.

5 CD1 55 Listen and colour the correct circle.

6 **Complete the face (☺). Colour the picture.**

7 Make a big toy and a small toy.

1

2

3

8 Say the toys. Colour the circles.

1

2

3

4

5 My numbers

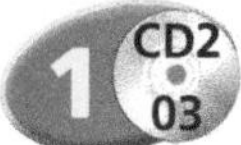

1 Listen and colour. Say the numbers.

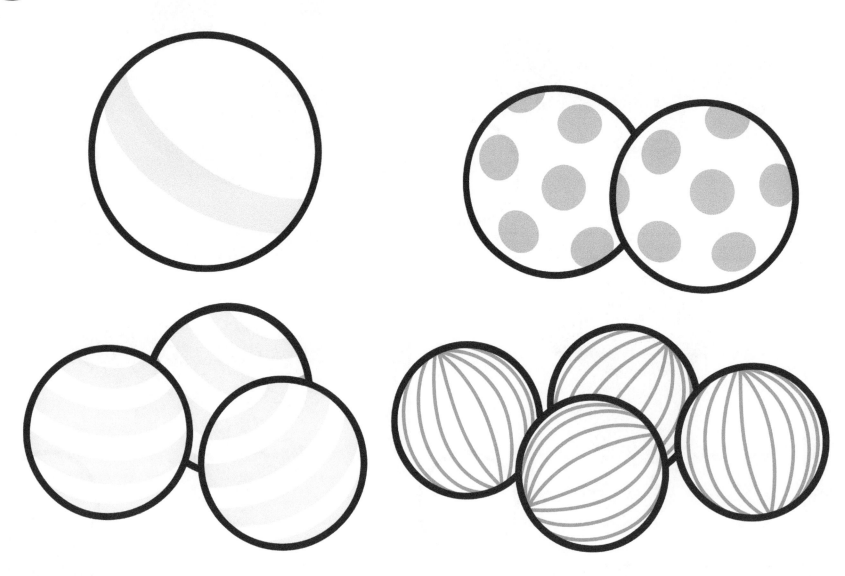

2 Look and circle. Say the sentences.

Listen and circle.

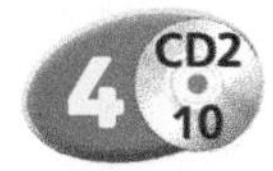

Listen again and colour.

Listen and colour the correct circle.

6 Complete the face (☺). Colour the picture.

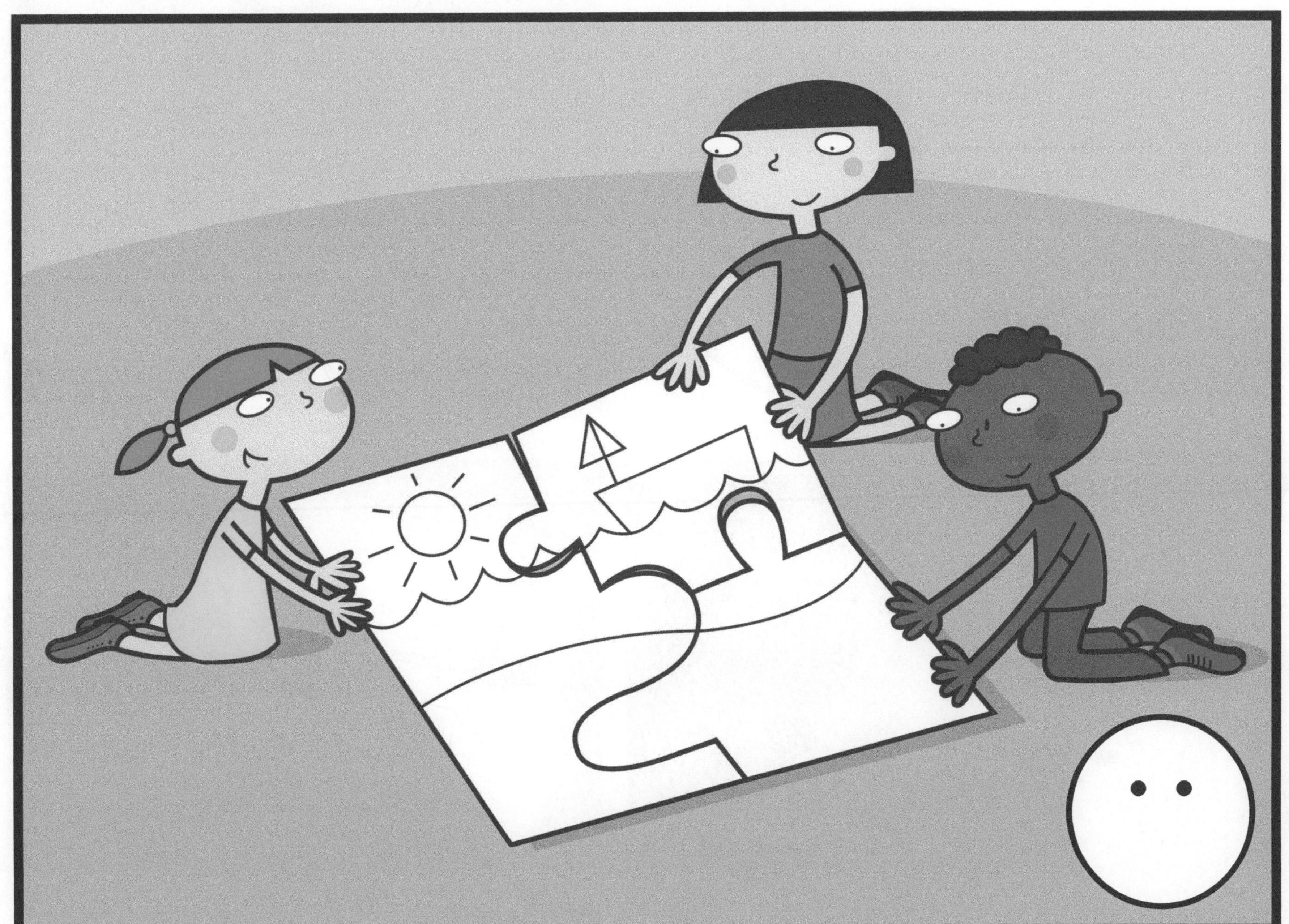

7 Make a number train.

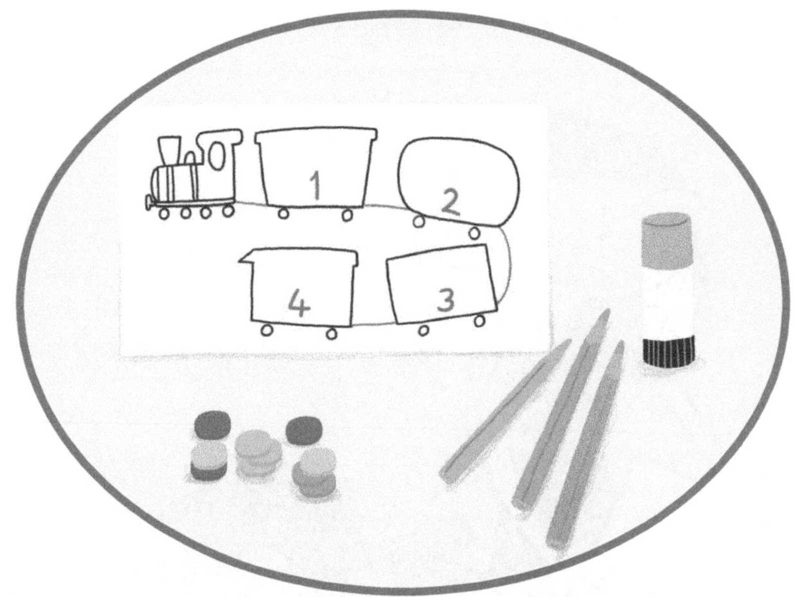

1

2

3

8 Say the numbers. Colour the circles.

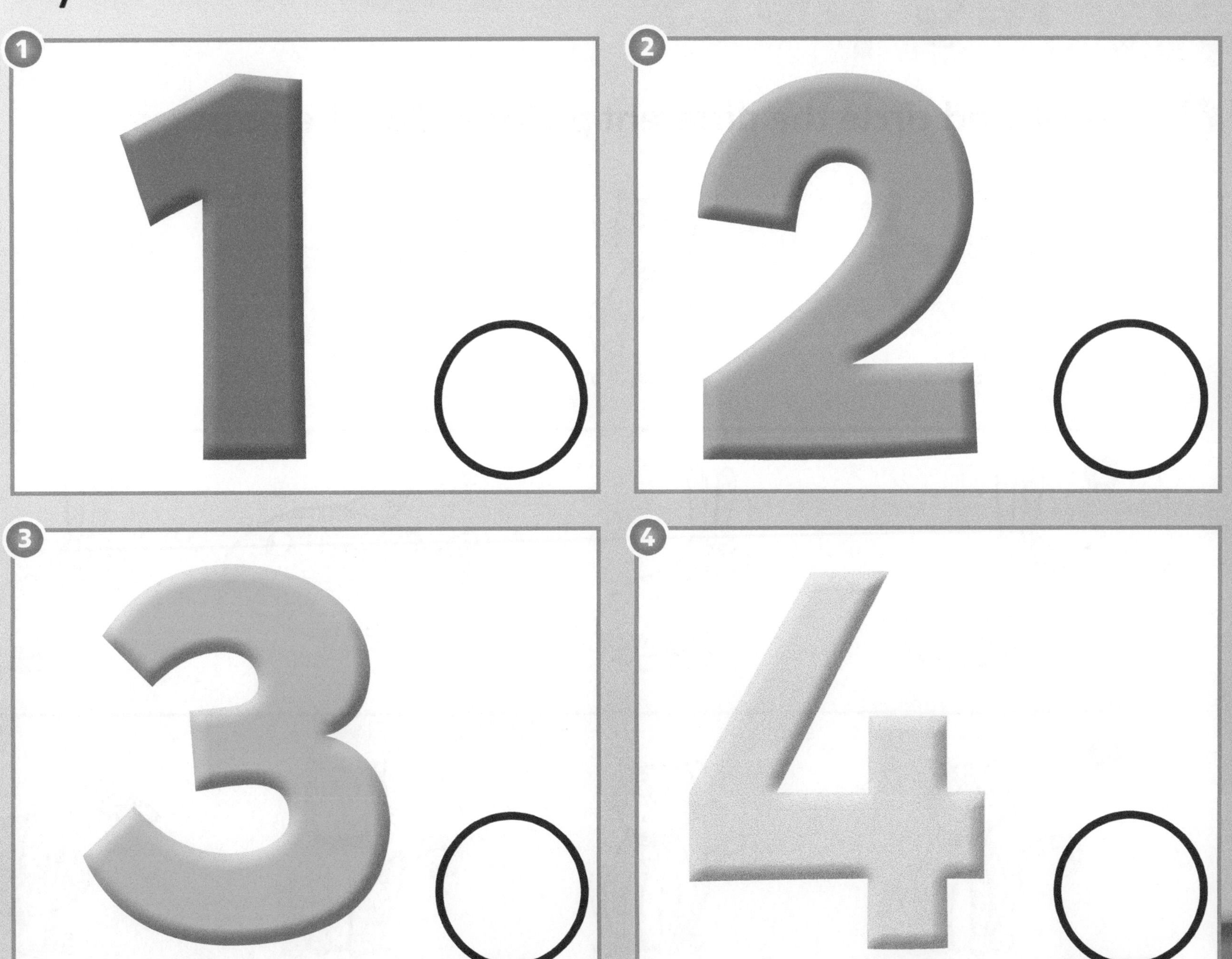

6 My pets

1 Look and circle the different pictures. Say the pets.

1

2

3

 bird, rabbit, fish, cat

Listen and join the dots. Say the sentence.

Listen and circle.

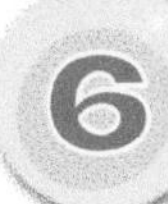

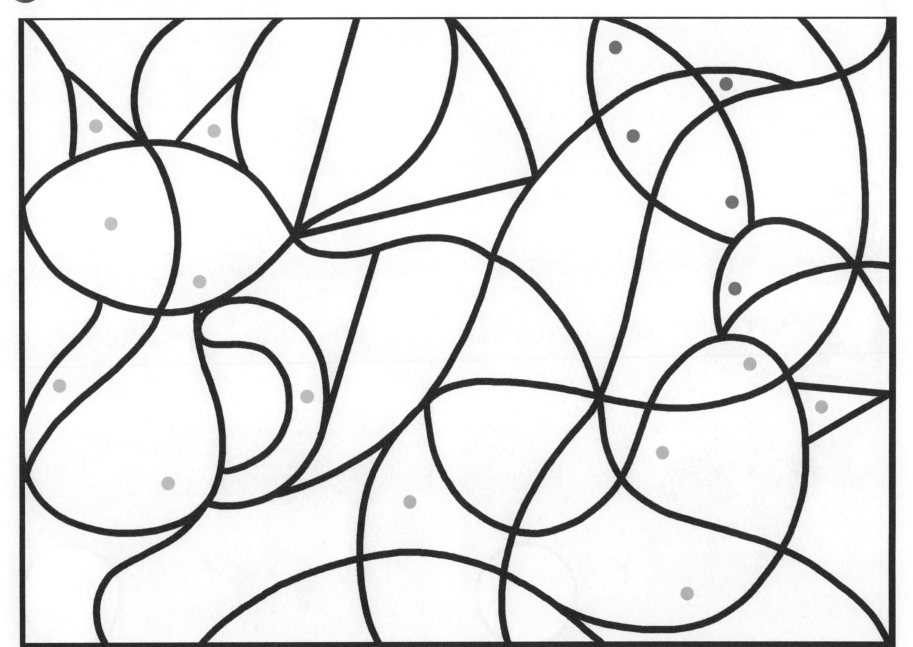

4 Look and colour.

5 CD2 25 Listen and colour the correct circle.

6 Complete the face (☺). Colour the picture.

7 Make a handprint bird.

1

2

3

8 Say the pets. Colour the circles.

1

2

3

4

7 My food

1 Look and match. Say the food.

 pasta, salad, rice, cake

2 **Draw something you like. Say the sentence.**

Listen and circle.

4 Follow the path.

5 CD2 36 Listen and colour the correct circles.

1

2

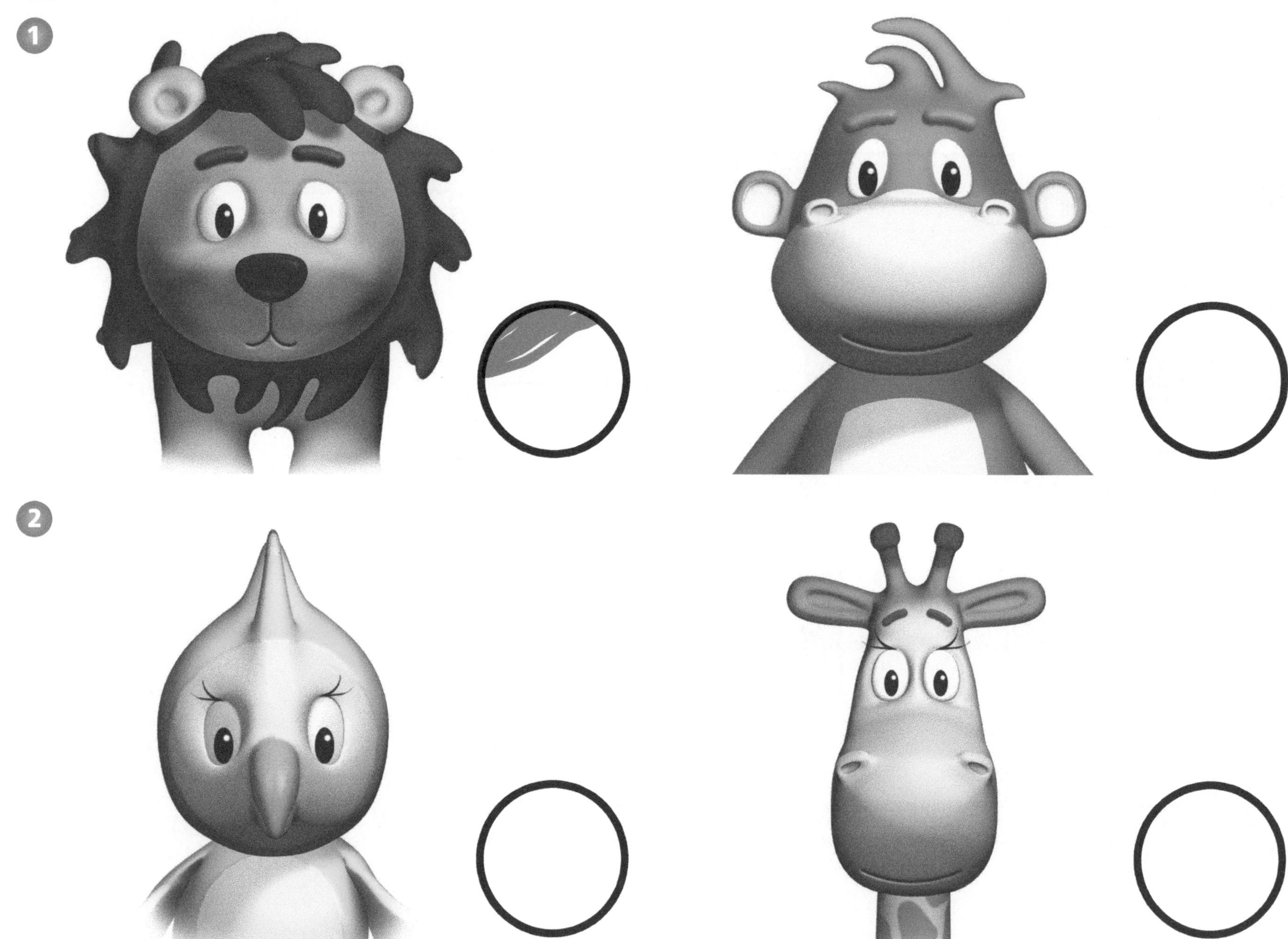

6 Complete the face (☺). Colour the picture.

7 Make a pasta fish.

1

2

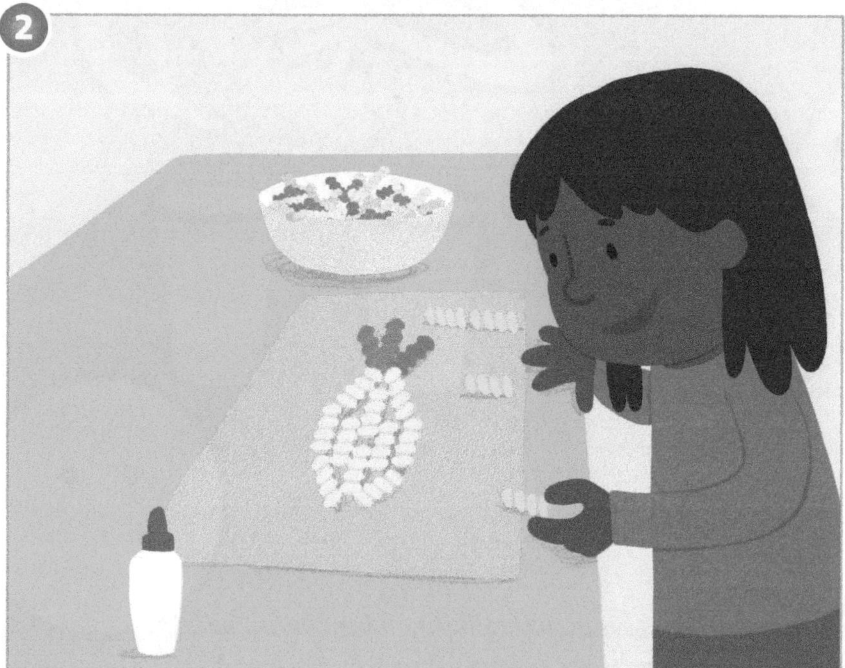

3

8 Say the food. Colour the circles.

1

2
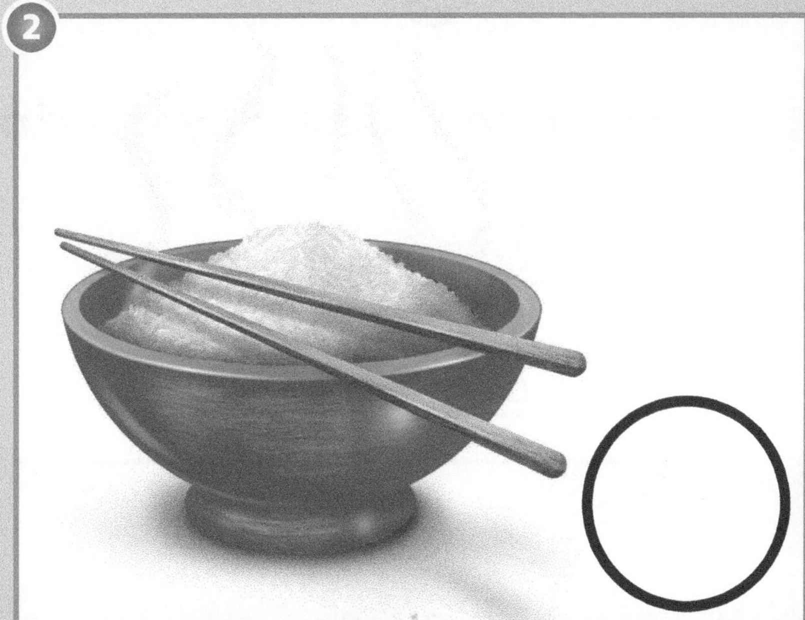

3

4

8 My clothes

1 Look and circle. Say the clothes.

Listen and cross (✗) the 'don't likes'. Say the sentences.

Listen and circle.

2

4 Look and match the children with their clothes.

5 CD2 49 Listen and colour the correct circles.

1

2

6 **Complete the face (☺). Colour the picture.**

7 Make a hat.

1

2

3

8 Say the clothes. Colour the circles.

1

2

3

4

9 My park

1 CD2 53 **Listen and colour. Say the words.**

1

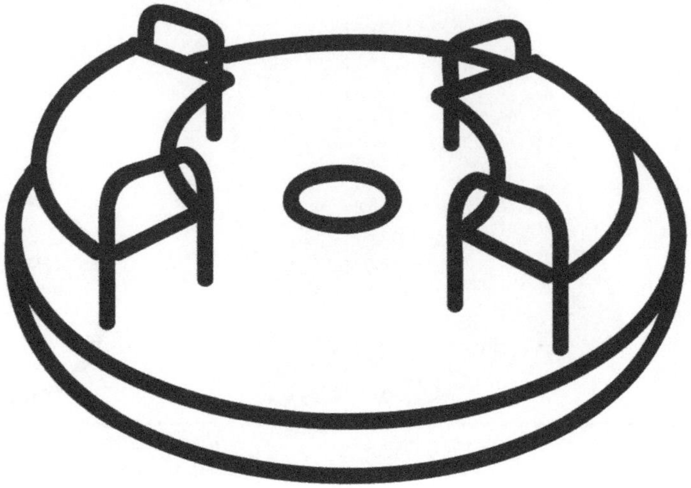

2

3

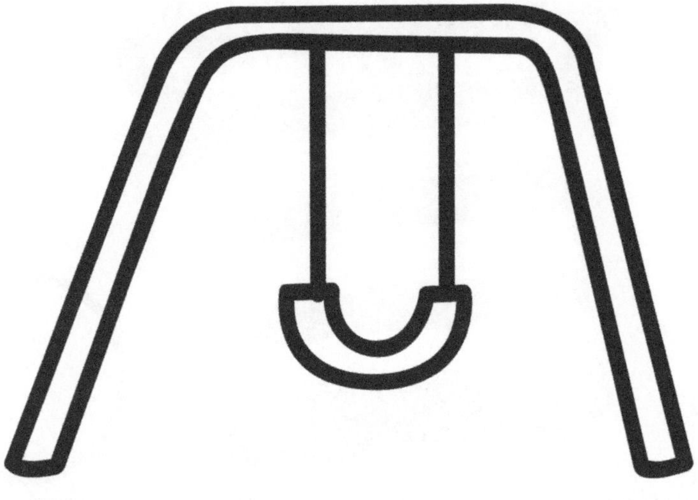

4

slide, roundabout, seesaw, swing

Listen and join the dots. Say the sentence.

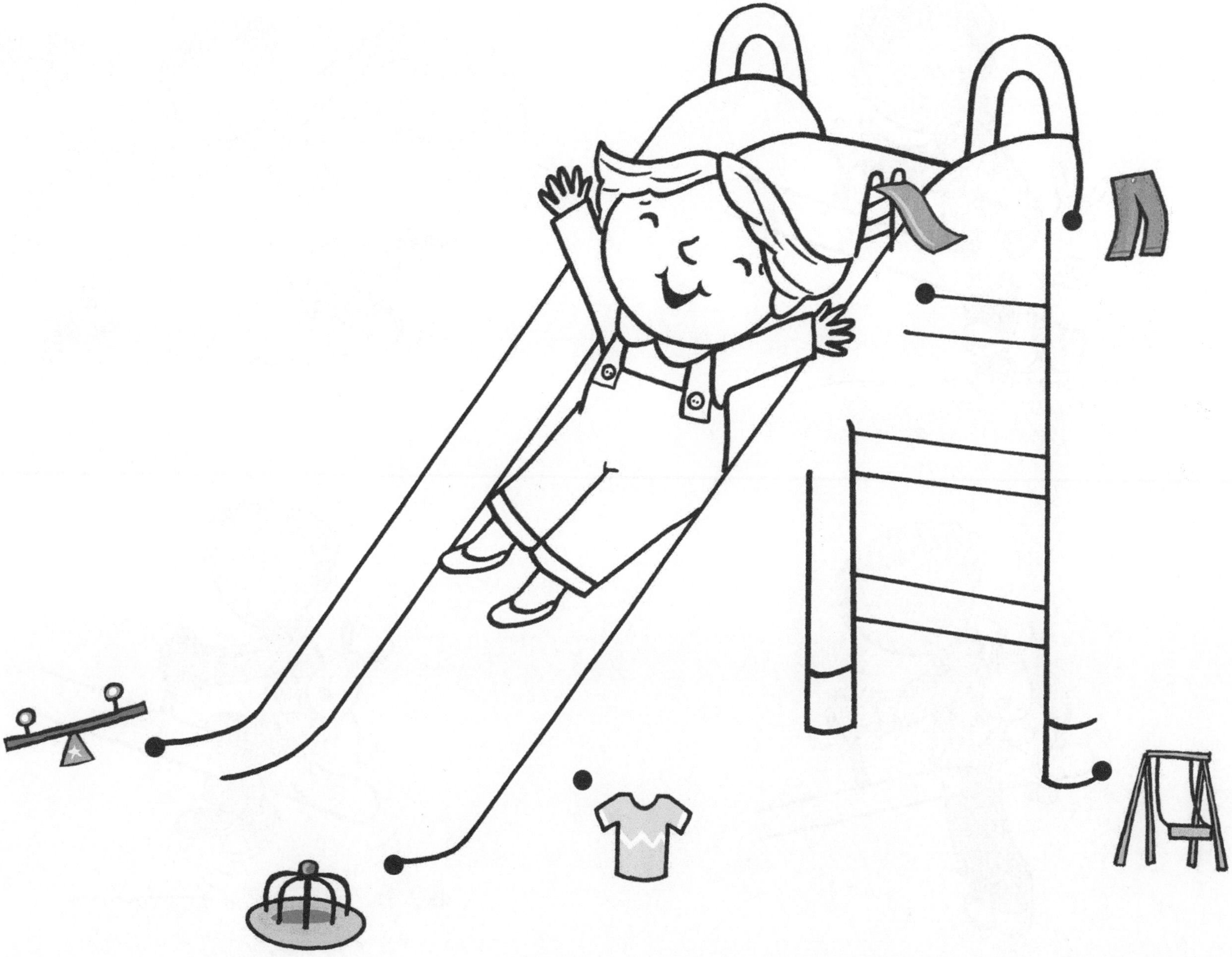

Listen and circle.

4 **Follow the path and count the swings.**

1 2 3 4

5 Listen and colour the correct circles.

1

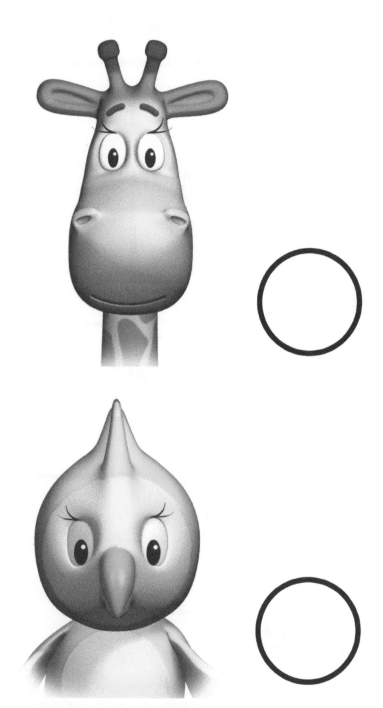

2

6 **Complete the face (☺). Colour the picture.**

7 Make a shapes cat.

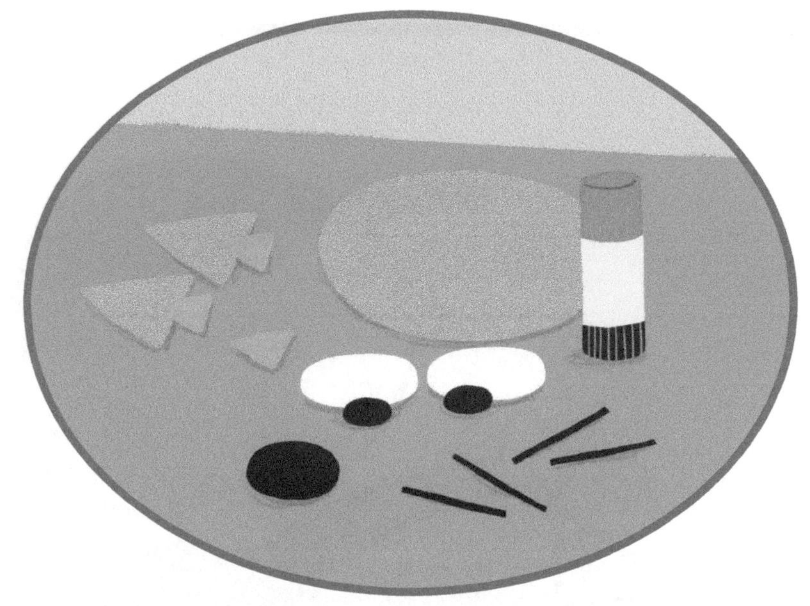

8 Say the words. Colour the circles.

1
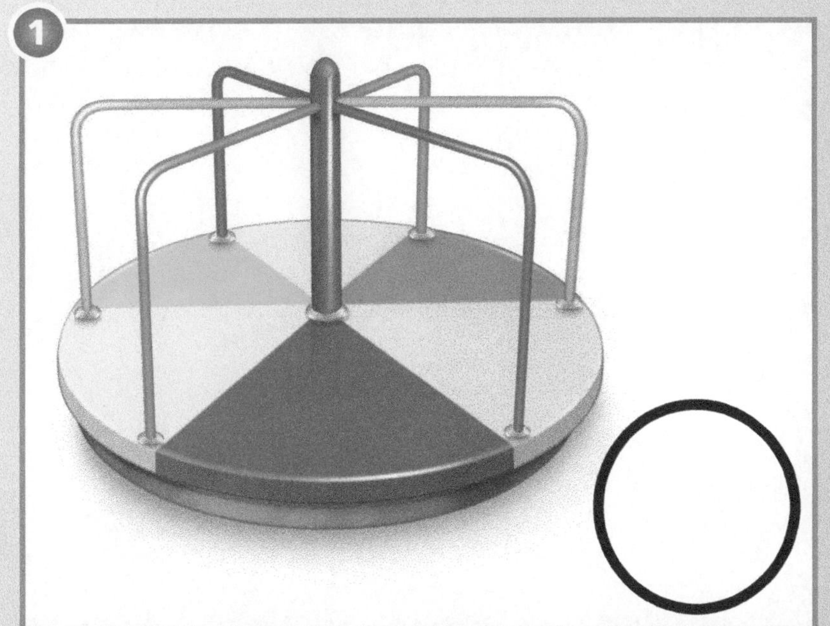

2
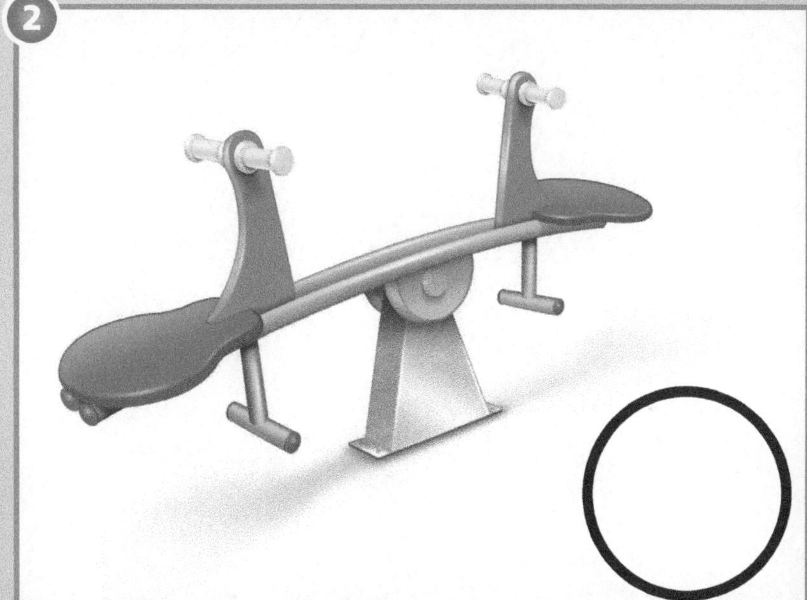

3

4

p
b
P

d
c

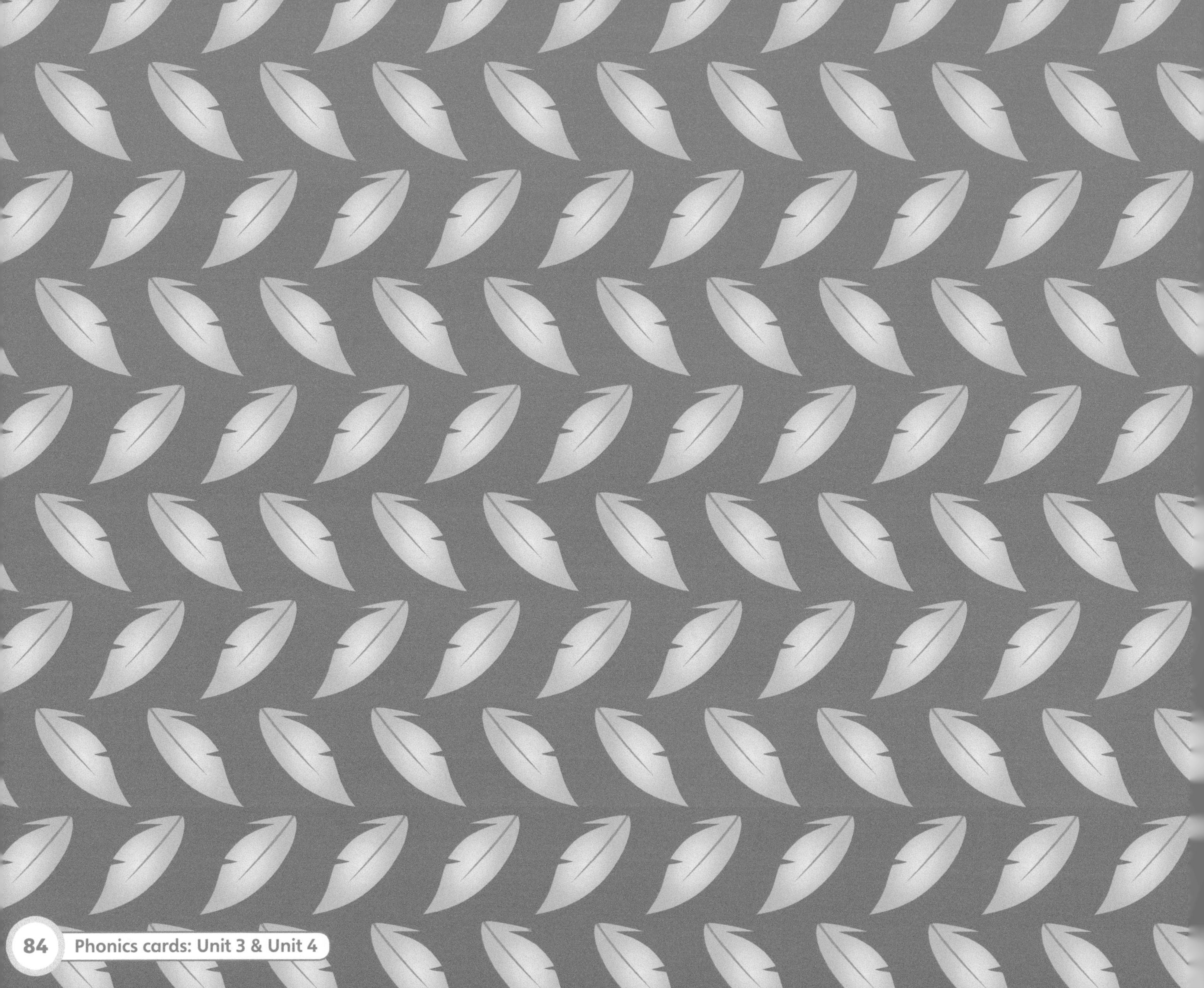

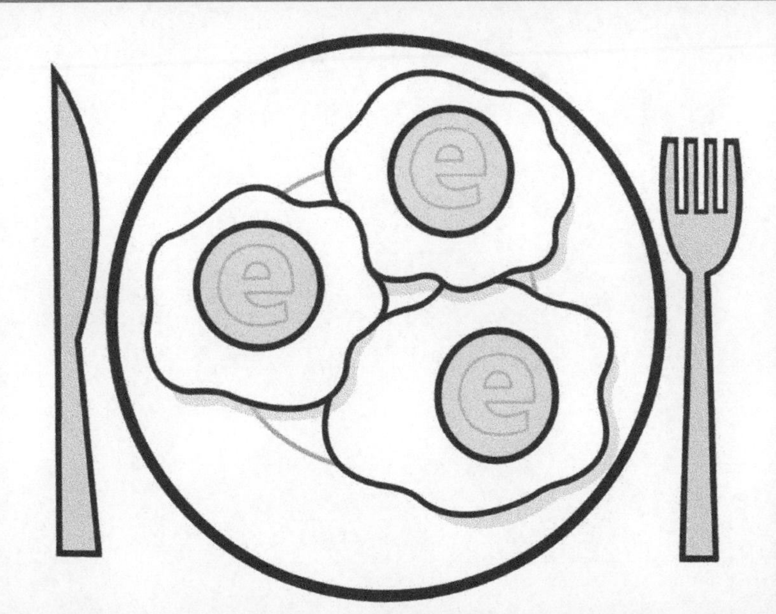

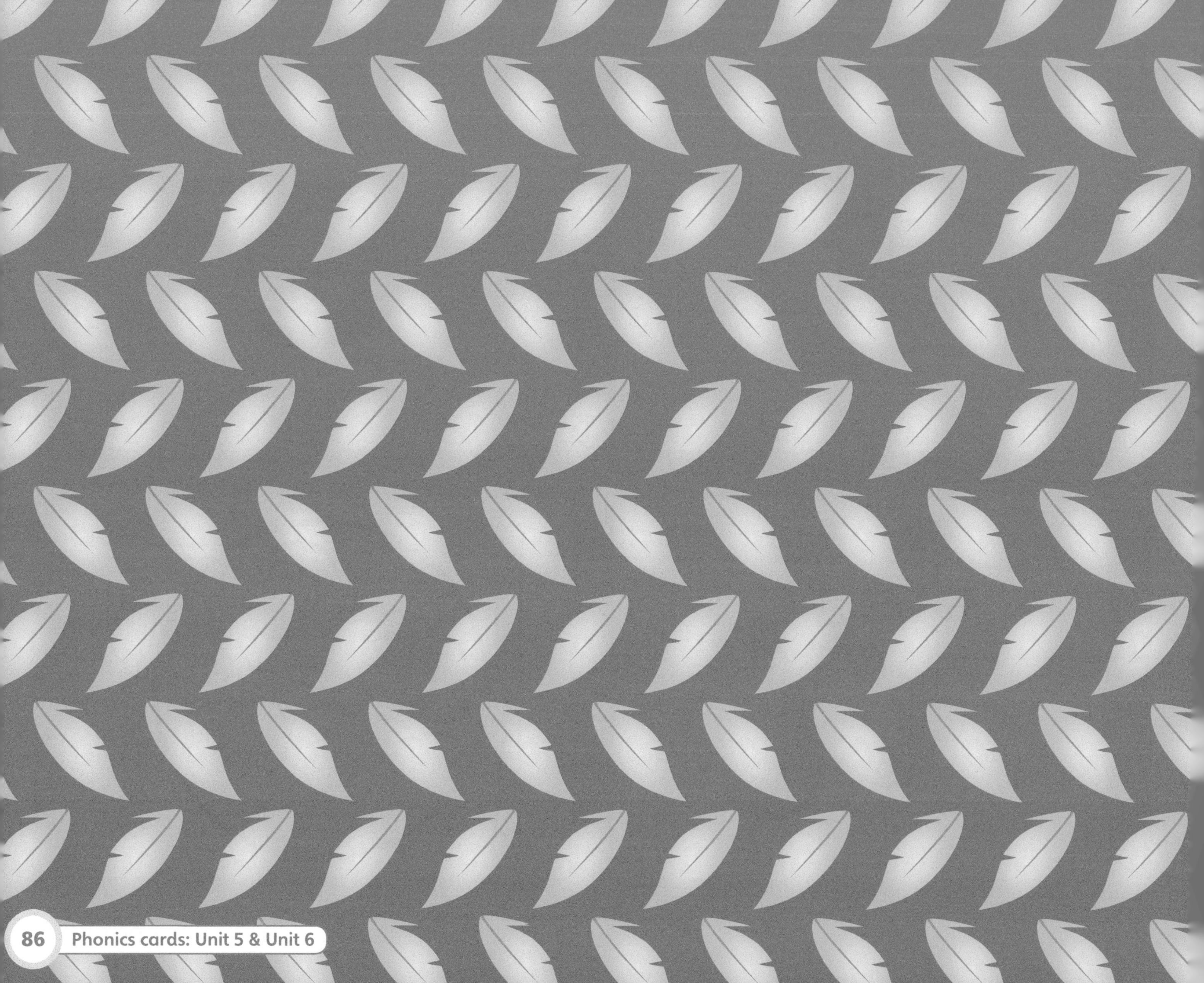

s

n

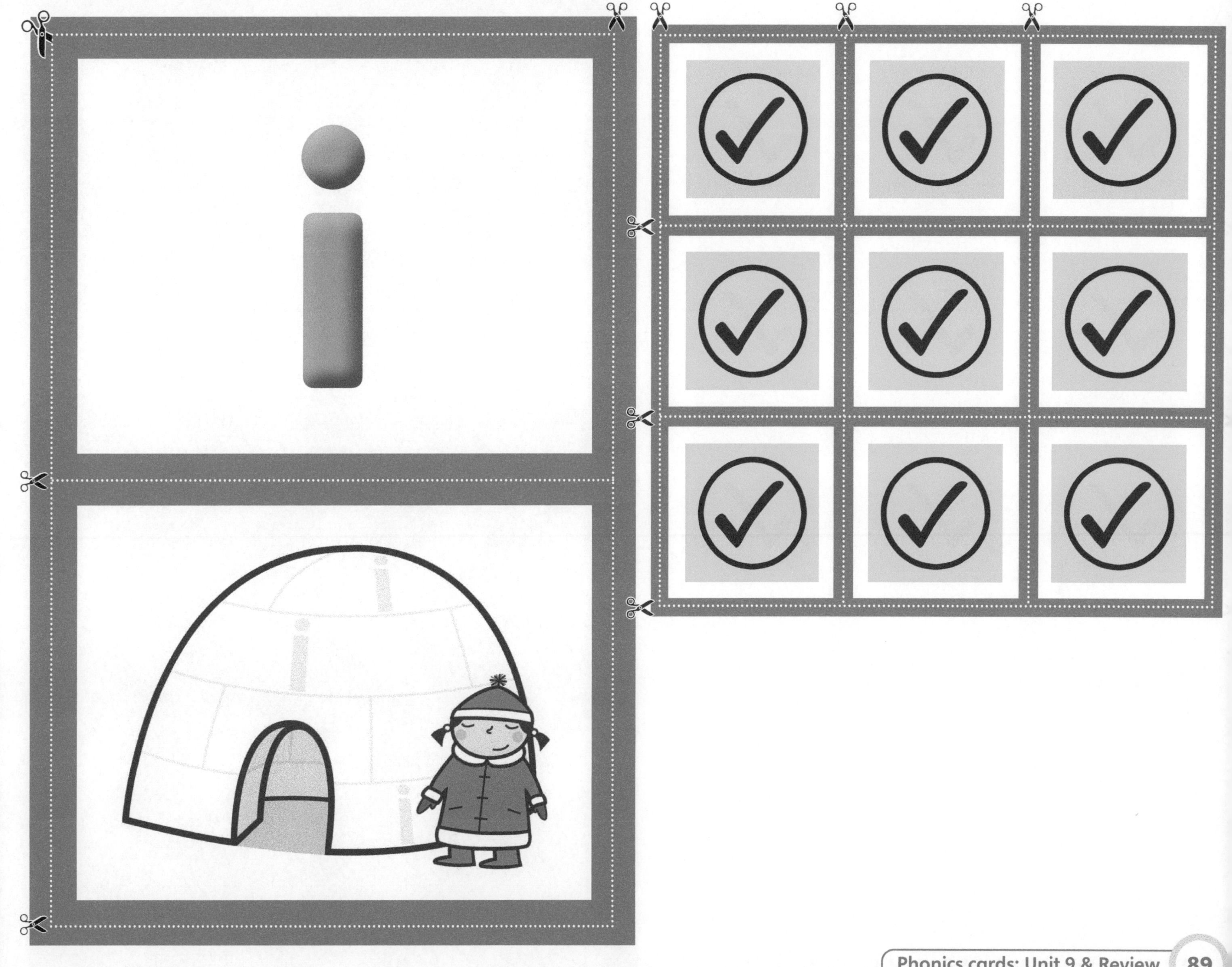
i

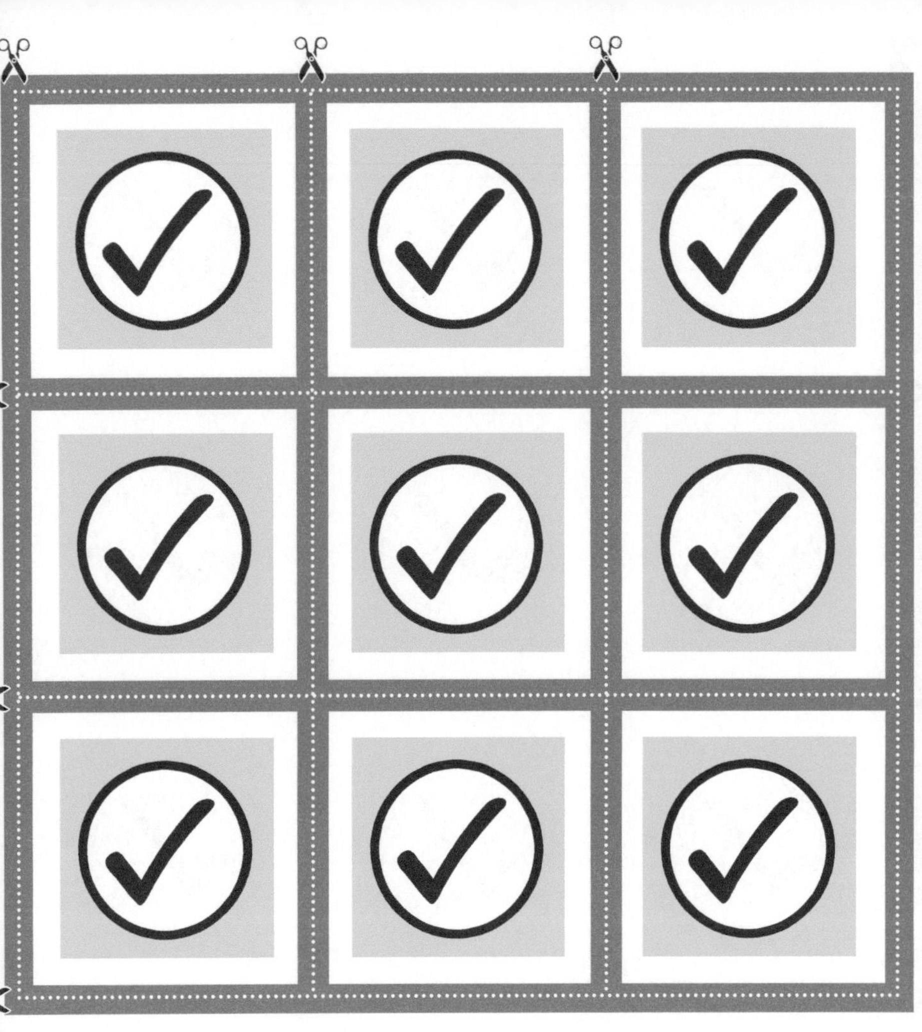

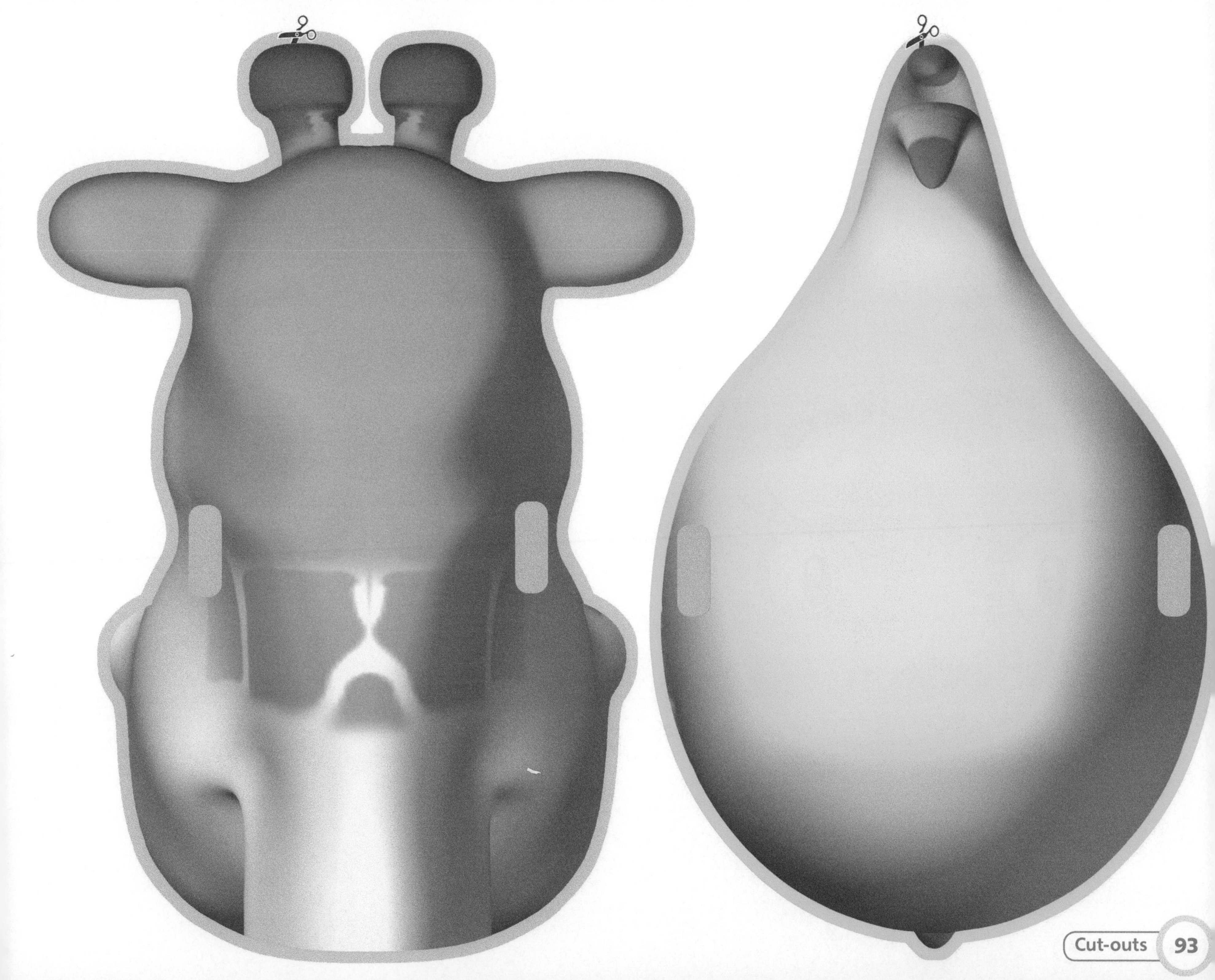

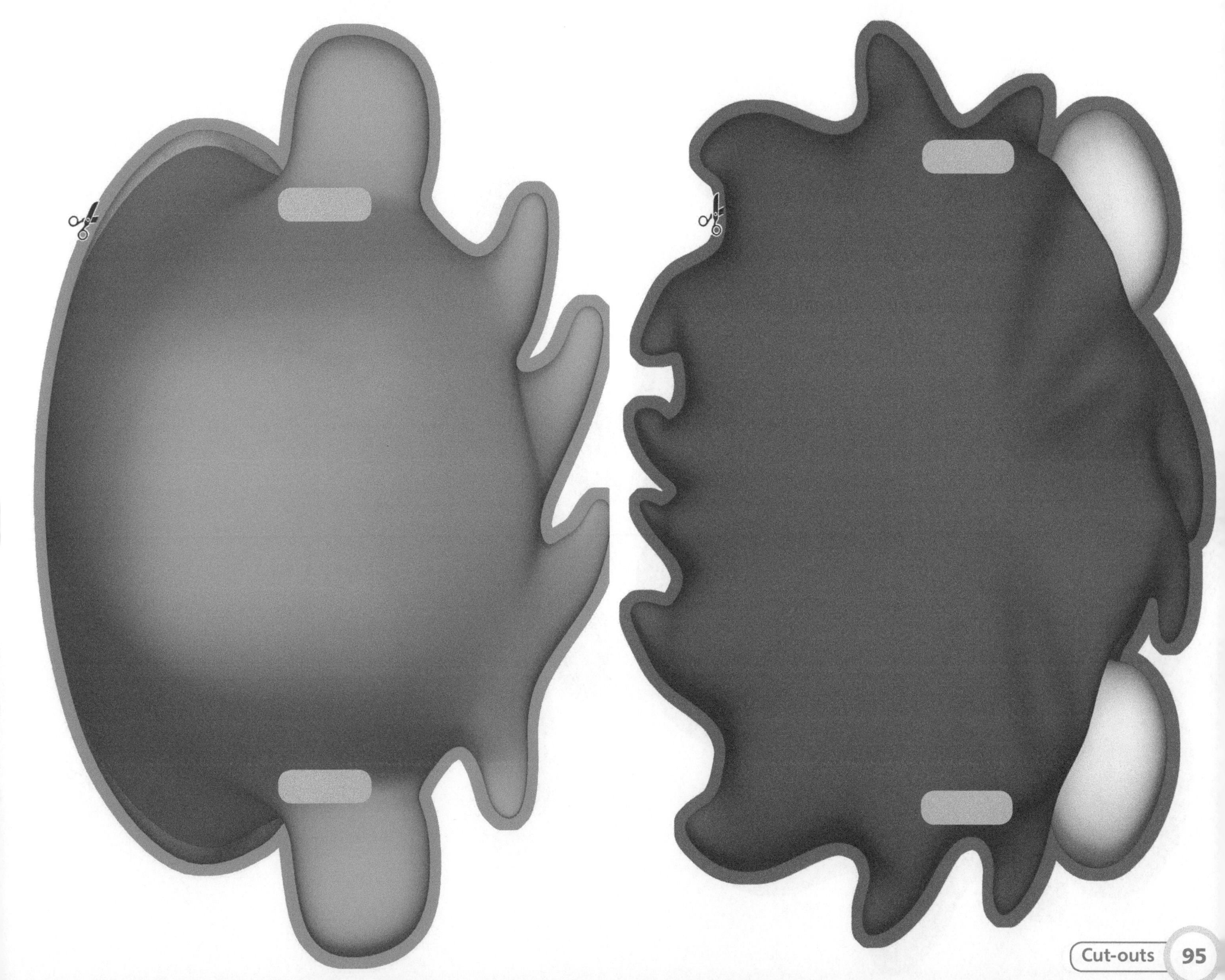

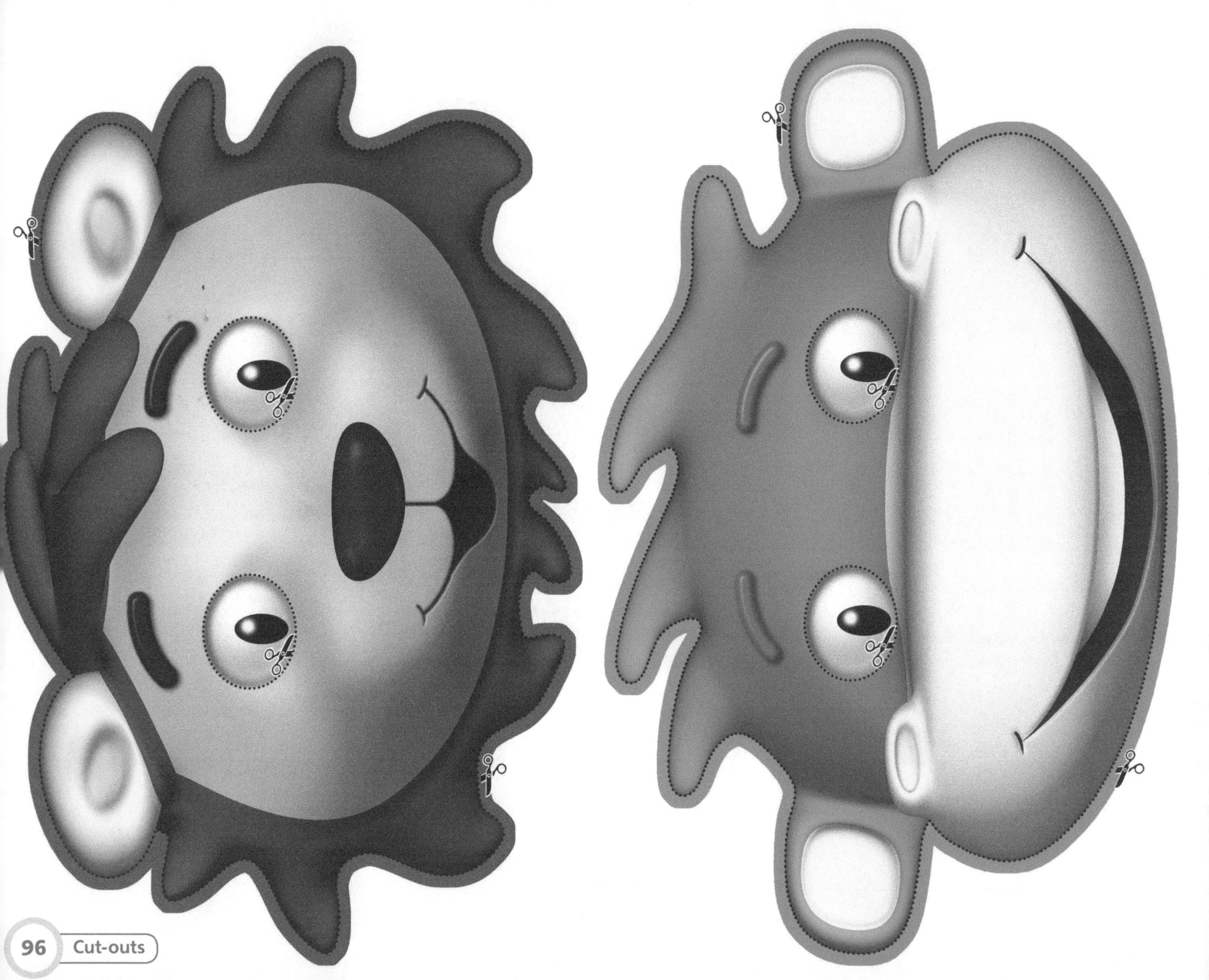